10 SECRETS TO EMPOWER KIDS & AWAKEN THE CHILD IN YOU

Written by Mark Papadas
President & Founder, The I Am 4 Kids Foundation

ISBN: 978-1-4751-4336-2

This book is a work of non-fiction. Unless specifically noted under Acknowledgements, all quotes and/or references to outside subject matter are made per copyright fair use law under commentary, educational and/or parody infusions within this work.

10 Secrets To Empower Kids & Awaken The Child In You

Up to a point a man's life is shaped by environment, heredity, and movements and changes in the world about him. Then there comes a time when it lies within his grasp to shape the clay of his life into the sort of thing he wishes to be. Only the weak blame parents, their race, their times, lack of good fortune, or the quirks of fate. Everyone has it within his power to say, ***"This I am today; that I will be tomorrow."*** ~Louis L'Amour, American author; 1908 – 1988

Table of Contents

Illustrations by Scott Kempler

"*This book is for any adult with kids in their life. It's for any of you who have the desire to empower your kids by helping them through the discovery process of deciding for themselves who they really are and realizing the potential they have inside.*

A name is only a label given to you by your parents and by you to your children. Who we are, who our kids are, is the sum of our beliefs, our values, our desires, goals and experiences.

This book is a tool enabling you to give the gift of The Power of True Identity to all of the kids in your life."

Mark Papadas

Acknowledgements

With a great deal of thanks and sincere gratitude I dedicate this book to those who taught and guided me through the creation of my own true identity...

Suzanne Papadas – My beautiful wife and the Love of My Life.

Nikki, Dani and Alex Papadas - The three Greatest Kids...ever.

Guy & Sheila Papadas - My parents and two great role models.

Terry & Kathy Travis – My best friends who have always been there for me.

Chuck Schultz – My good friend and old radio show co-host.

All of my friends at **Engaging Speakers, Positive Charge**, and the **Power Team** who encouraged me when I decided to change my focus and work exclusively with kids.

Earl Nightingale, Brian Tracy & Tony Robbins – Three men whose work and passion have shown me how to open my mind and let the creativity flow.

Pat Walsh – A conversation with a friend turned into an epiphany of creativity and discovery.

And finally, **THANK YOU** for taking this book in hand. My sincerest hope and desire is that this tool helps you guide your children, grandchildren, brothers, sisters, nieces, nephews, students, little leaguers, all the kids in your life to finding The Power of Their True Identities!

This book is also to awaken the kid in everyone! Live your life with the passion of a kid. Jump in puddles! Live like its play! Learn something new!

Together, let's bring out the kid in everyone!

Make A Difference EVERY Day,
Mark Papadas

COMPLETE THIS PHRASE BEFORE PROCEEDING
(Write your answer directly on this page)

I AM...

Stuck.

Introduction

How did you finish that statement?

Was your answer long or short?

Was your language positive or negative?

Did you write something simple like, 'I AM... a winner or loser'?

Did you even bother to write an answer or did you just decide to read the next page?

I put you through this exercise first so that you can do it with your kids. Grab a blank piece of paper and write I Am... at the top and ask your kids to complete it no matter their age. If they look at you a little funny, just tell them it's a project from a book you're reading and that they'll be helping you get to the next step.

How you complete the statement, I AM... says everything about who you are. It speaks volumes about the standards you have for yourself and what you expect from others. It shows how you live your life.

The words you choose to write about yourself reflect how you've been living. If you used negative wording you might be spending a lot of time getting lost in problems and challenges. You're most likely worrying, being upset, unsatisfied, complaining, feeling depressed about things that, later on, you might discover aren't all that important after all. You're exhausting a lot of negative energy.

If you used positive wording you might be spending a lot of time exploring alternative options and finding solutions to problems. You might worry about the occasional unexpected situation that pops up, but don't really sweat the small stuff.

You're more likely to find a way to deal with things. You're creating a lot of positive energy.

How you finish the phrase, I Am... determines the quality of your life and the lives of everyone around you. It's actually an attitude, a personal philosophy and belief system that guides you in every decision you make. It is the essence of who you are. It is your identity. The key question is: Do YOU know who YOU are?

Have YOU decided on your identity? If you haven't, you're letting others decide for you. Is that really what you want for YOUR life or do you want to be the one who decides what you do and how you feel?

Guess what... Falling into the trap of being who others tell you to be (or who you think they want you to be) because it's what you've always been told, is not your fault. Only a small percentage of people in the world today have ever given it any thought. Most people have never been asked to consider the idea of who they really are. As a result, people usually have not established goals let alone a process for achieving them. You may have dreams. You may have wishes. But, those aren't goals.

A lot of people have no specific plan, living day to day and paycheck to paycheck. Bouncing between the events that happen in their lives they live like a pinball being randomly hit by bumpers in the game of life and ask themselves, *"Why does this always happen to me?"* That's a tough way to exist.

And, for generations people have been told that when you grow up, you get a job, start a family, raise kids, become a grandparent, retire, end of story. Just doing something because you're "supposed to" ... Why?

Most of the time when you first meet someone you ask them who they are. The response is almost always their name and what it is they do for a living. But is a name or a job really who someone *"is"*?

Would Mother Theresa have been a different person if her name was Sue? No. Mother Theresa didn't move through life being 'Mother Theresa'. No. She moved through life being caring, supportive, loving, compassionate and knowledgeable, all according to her faith. All parts of her identity that she chose to express each day.

"One of the greatest diseases is to be nobody to anybody." ~ Mother Teresa

People are complex. Our bodies are made up of multiple intricate systems that work together seamlessly, at least most of the time. All of this is controlled by our brain, the most powerful processing tool ever. It controls every function of our body without requiring conscious thought. It shouldn't be any surprise then that the answer to *'who are you'* isn't always given much conscious thought.

But, the ones who have given this idea some deliberation are some of the most successful people in the world today.

I'll walk you through a simple process for establishing an identity that will empower you and your kids to achieve goals that you thought were impossible. I heard Dr. Robert Schuler once ask, *"What would you attempt if you knew you could not fail?"*

Right here, right now, I challenge you to finish this process as soon as possible. Every day that you go through life without your true identity is a day that you will never get back. No more procrastinating. No more time wasting. It's time to discover who you are!

A wise person once said, *"Yesterday is history. Tomorrow is a mystery. Today is a gift. That's why we call it the present."*

Let's open your gift and get started!

I Am...

Chapter 1

Decide It!

*"I am the miracle" ~ Hindu Prince Gautama Siddharta
~ Founder of Buddhism 563 – 483 BC*

Who do you want to be? It's the title of a song that was originally released in 1983 by the rock band Oingo Boingo. It's an upbeat, kind of silly song. But it asks a very important question.

Who do I want to BE today?

It's the first question you need to ask yourself every day. It's a simple question with an endless variety of answers that can be expressed in countless ways. All you have to do is make a decision.

Who do I want to BE today? Decide it!

The word 'decision' originally and literally means 'to-cut-off-from.' Think back to some important decisions you've made in your life. I'm not talking about soup or salad, paper or plastic, or other every day choices. I'm talking about serious decisions that affected your life and others.

Once you make a decision, once you decide, there are no other options. You have cut off all other possibilities. Success is your only option. Failure... is not!

Who do you want to BE today? The great thing about this question is that there is no right or wrong answer..., only a process for getting YOUR answer. The past only equals the present, not the future.

The rest of your life is like a movie in production. You are about to create the script and act out the characters and events. Some scenes will be improvised. You can't control everything that happens in the course of your life, but you can control how you respond. Just make sure you "*stay in character*."

Let's start by building the foundation of your Identity. You're about to design your own personal role model. Pick and choose the best parts of people you admire, real or fictional. Here in this book write as many as you can think of. There is NO LIMIT to who you can become!

OK grown-ups, call in your kids and review these questions with them. And remember, you should answer these too. Discovering your identity is just as important as helping your kids discover theirs. Besides, your kids are going to ask you. Don't you think you should have an answer?

Who are my role models?
(*Note: If you don't have good role models, make some up*)

Who influences me?

Who would I like to impress?

Who would it hurt if I disappointed them?

Who has already achieved a goal I have set for myself?

Who would I like to be friends with?

Who would I like to be in a relationship with?

If I'm already in a relationship so, how can I make it better?

What are my role model's goals and how have they achieved them?

If you have the opportunity, interview the people you chose as role models.
Share with them what you're doing and why you're doing it. Tell them why you've chosen them as role models and what about them you would like to emulate. Explain that you don't want to BE them but that you admire some of their traits. Find out everything you can. Ask how, why, who, what and where they adopted those traits.

To help you get your interviews rolling, here are a few questions you can ask:

How did you...?

How do you feel about...?

What made you...?

What were you thinking when you...?

What does that mean?

Why is/was that important?

Why did you...?

Who did you get advice from?

Who else should I talk to about...?

Keep digging. Don't stop with the first answer you are given. Ask for more answers. You'll find this will not only benefit you, but will often be a great opportunity for the role models to reflect on their own identity as well.

If you can't interview (*for whatever reason*) your role model, then picture the interview in your mind. Ask your questions and imagine their answers.

There is one rule to follow when conducting these interviews: You may NOT accept the answer, "I DON'T KNOW" in any form. Be sure to share this rule with the person you're interviewing before you begin.

The phrase, 'I don't know' is actually a command to the brain of the person who says/thinks it. It tells the brain that it doesn't know the answer and locks down your thinking system. Whether you're sitting across from your father or picturing yourself with your childhood idol, ask the following question **exactly** as follows:

"I know you don't know and that's OK. But if you did know, what would the answer be?"

This question acts like a password to unlock the brain. It gives your brain permission to find the answer to any question.

It's interesting that our brains are a lot like computers. Not in a free thinking imaginative way, but in the way that they must and will only do what they are told to do. In fact, it's nearly impossible for your brain to work with negative commands.

Take this command for example: Do **NOT** think of a silly clown riding a giant pink elephant in a parade down Main Street while a monkey sits atop the clown's head.

What did you just do?

You pictured a monkey sitting on the head of a silly clown riding a giant pink elephant down Main Street. And, even though it wasn't specified, you most likely filled in the imagery for Main Street with the Main Street that runs through your town. You thought of all of this even though the command was specifically NOT to think of any of it.

The fact is, our brains have to go and find what it is they're being told NOT to do in order NOT to do it. It's a unique positive paradox.

Go ahead and give it a try. On the next page write the answer to a question that you don't know how to answer. Do it by giving yourself permission to discover the answer.

I know I don't know the answer to this question and that's OK:
(*Write your question here.*)

But if I did know, what would the answer be?
(*Write your answer. It doesn't matter what it is, just write it.*)

Chapter 2

Write It!

"We have all a better guide in ourselves, if we would attend to it, than any other person can be." ~ Jane Austen, English novelist; 1775 – 1817

OK, it's true; I'm getting off a little easy here. Why? It's because YOU are going to write this chapter of the book. Only you can create your true identity. All I can do is provide you with the tools you need to make it happen. Like any other piece of art, you'll have many drafts and versions of your identity before it's completed.

The opening of page of this book was your first draft. Remember? When you completed the statement, I AM...

Take a look back at the people and their traits you chose to emulate in Chapter 1. I'll bet it's a pretty impressive list. Now, on the following pages, write down, in painstaking detail, what you admire most about those people.

Let your mind and pen run wild. Come up with as many things as you can. If you don't have at least 25 things, you're not trying hard enough.

The questions at the top of the next few pages will help guide you...

What are the things that make me like them?

How do they think?

What do they do?

What are their character traits?

What behavior patterns or physical characteristics would I like to emulate?

What skills do they have that I'd like to possess?

This is your outline. Review what you've just written. This is the foundation of the identity you are creating. And, like all foundations, this is where the building really starts. What comes next?

Ask yourself the question, *"What else?"* If you come up with an answer, then go back and add it to your list. Keep going until you can no longer answer the *"what else"* question. Now you're ready to start writing your identity.

With the exception of the words, "I AM..." the following pages have been left blank for you. You are free to use any form you choose to represent your identity. Use words, pictures, drawings, colors, whatever moves you.

Use bullet points or flowery prose. It's your choice. Do what works for you. You have a blank canvas.

There are three simple but important rules to follow:

❖ Express everything in the present tense. I AM..., not I Will or I Want.
  ➢ Example: **I AM...** a giving person who prospers by helping others prosper.

❖ Express everything as if it has already been achieved, with a possible caveat at the end to show progress.
  ➢ Example: **I AM...** a Billionaire whose accounts are in the process of being fully funded.

❖ Express everything using positive language. You can address negative topics; you just need to use language in the correct way. This is about who you ARE, not who you aren't.
  ➢ Example: **I AM...** a non-smoker rather than **I AM... NOT** a smoker.

I AM...

I AM...

I AM...

I AM...

Chapter 3

Improve It!

"I am my own heroine" ~ Marie Bashkirtseff, Russian author of the diary 'I Am The Most Interesting Book of All'; 1858 – 1954

Now that you've created an identity, it's time to improve it. People are capable of anything we decide to accomplish. It's just a question of how hard and how long we are willing to work to create the changes we want.

A wise man once said to me, *"Everywhere is within walking distance... if you have the time."* So, how far are you willing to walk?

Why only do what others have already accomplished? Why not aim higher? Why be good when you can be GREAT!? Why be great when you can be the BEST!?

For example:
- ❖ Why seek a work/life balance when you'd rather retire to spend time with your family sitting by the pool at your beach house?

- ❖ Why look for "A" relationship when you can have "THE" relationship?

Now, re-write your identity with these improvements. Let your mind run wild. Who would you be and what would you do if there was no chance of failure? What would you write or draw if all you had to do to make it come true was to put it on paper? Write it on the following pages.

I AM...

I AM...

I AM...

I AM...

I AM...

Chapter 4
Believe & Reinforce It!

"And remember, no matter where you go, there you are." ~ Confucius, Chinese philosopher; 551BC – 479BC

This step is the moment of truth. *"It's where the rubber meets the road."* If you don't believe 100% in your mind and body that the identity you just forged **IS** who you are, then you will never live up to it.

Belief in who you are is crucial to establishing your identity. Maybe you're not sure what I mean by that. So, let's take a look at what a belief *is?*

The dictionary definition of 'Belief' is, *"acceptance by the mind that something is true or real, often underpinned by an emotional or spiritual sense of certainty."*

That's a lot of information to break down for such a short statement, but it is important to understand how it all works for you to get the most out of this process. Let's break down the definition piece by piece.

1. *"Acceptance by the mind that something is true or real"*: Our mind cannot tell the difference between something it imagines and believes with conviction and something that is *"real."*

Subconsciously, we do this all the time. For example: Have you ever spoken on the phone with someone you have never met? In your mind's eye, you have a picture of what this person looks like. Based on your conversations and the sounds of his/her voice, you start to make judgments about what type of person he/she is. Until you actually meet them in person, the image of her that your mind's eye has created is your reality.

Understanding this, you can consciously tell your brain and body to define what is true and real to you. Your new identity will be as true and real as you make it.

2. *"Underpinned by an emotional or spiritual sense"*: We are emotional creatures. We trust our beliefs because it makes us feel a certain way when we do: Sometimes good and sometimes bad; sometimes safe and secure and sometimes frightened and unsure. The stronger the emotional connection to an idea, the stronger the belief.

Everything we do is based upon how it makes us feel. Most people don't realize that emotions are directly related to our physical health and wellbeing. There are physical patterns coordinated by your body making connections in the brain. In other words, emotions are not something you think, they are something you **DO**. This is part of the Mind/Body connection.

In the next chapter I'll show you how to embed your identity into your physiological DNA.

3. *"of certainty"*: In psychology, there is a hierarchy of six Human Needs. The feeling of *"certainty"* is the #1 psychological need for every human being. The feeling of control or knowing what comes next makes us feel comfortable and allows us to experience a wide variety of things.

I know a lot of adults reading this book might be familiar with Abraham Maslow's Hierarchy of Five Basic Human Needs. For those of you who aren't familiar with Abraham Maslow, he founded the philosophy of Humanistic Psychology and before dying at the young age of 62, had been a psychology professor at Cornell University, Brooklyn College and Brandeis University.

In part, Maslow's Hierarchy of Five Human Needs coincide with the 6 core psychological needs. To better understand where 'Certainty' falls, I'll match these up for you.

Maslow's 5	Psychology's 6
1. Physiological	1. Certainty
2. Safety	2. Uncertainty
3. Love & Belonging	4. Love & Connection
4. Esteem	3. Significance
5. Self Actualization	5. Growth & 6. Contribution

As simple lists, you can see how these match up. Here, we're talking about belief and the importance of the certainty it creates. The safety established within the true acceptance of your identity.

Certainty equates to safety because we find safety within the certainty of our environment. We also create safety by dealing with the uncertainty of situations that come up that are not within our control.

What people don't often realize is that needs are often tied to addictions. The need to be loved, to be enough, to be smart. If something fills three or more psychological needs it can become an addiction.

Fear is another form of a belief. Fear is a negative belief that keeps us from doing what need to do to be successful. Fear is paralyzing force...

There's the fear of not being enough and the fear of not being loved. They're they most basic and powerful of fears.

With kids, there's the fear not being smart enough. They'll often doubt an answer they've come up with and won't raise their hand thinking, "everyone will laugh at you" ...

Take that fear based belief and associate it with something different. Thomas Edison was once asked by a reporter why he didn't give up on inventing the light bulb after 2,000 different experiments. "I was never discouraged. I was excited to discover 1,999 ways that didn't work!" Enjoying failures helps you get failure out of the way so you can move forward to getting the right answer. I'll come back to this later I the book.

A perfect example of certainty is how kids watch movies. How many times will a kid watch the same movie, TV show or DVD? 10? 100? 500? They do that because it is their way of attaining certainty and asserting a level of control of their situation and surroundings. Kids know that every time Nemo goes up to the boat, the scuba diver is going to come up from the bottom of the screen and put him in the little baggy.

As adults, our need of certainty is filled in a variety of more complicated ways, but the end result is the same. We do things to reach that feeling of certainty, even if the end result is not desirable.

Have you ever seen someone sabotage a relationship when it was going well? Have you ever seen someone mess up at work just before a promotion was coming? Have you ever seen an athlete "choke" under pressure and miss something he/she had done thousands of times before? Was that person you?

So, by definition, once you accept your identity and are certain of who you are, your mind will believe that the identity you've created is the real you. You will believe it deeply, passionately, and will discover a new sense of control in the certainty of who you are, in the certainty of what makes you, you.

To sum up, you get to decide what you believe. So you might as well have a belief that is going to empower you to achieve your goals. Decide to have great belief in yourself, in your identity.

Now that we've established what a belief is, we need to walk through the Belief Cycle and how it directly relates to certainty.

I don't know about you, but I like to be right. I enjoy success. In my mind, achievement of my goals is the only option because that is part of my identity. However, not everyone shares my optimistic outlook. They haven't been exposed to the science that you are learning within this book and applying to your life.

Most people don't know they can change anything they want about themselves, their education, or their business. People often tell me that if they start to see different results or a change, only then they will believe in something different. Unfortunately, it doesn't work that way.

Let's walk through the cycle.
- ❖ It all starts with a belief. You decide what you believe. Up to this point, your subconscious mind has been in control of this section of your life. Now, you get to consciously decide your reality. Why not decide on a great one?
- ❖ Once a belief is expressed, either consciously or subconsciously, the brain will determine the potential and then search out, find, and/or create the necessary resources to make the belief true. If the belief is a limiting belief that leads to detrimental outcomes, the brain will find all the things that will make that happen. But, if the belief is an empowering belief that leads to positive outcomes, it will find all those things too. That's why the questions you ask yourself and the language you use is so important when formulating your identity and goals.
- ❖ Based on the potential and resources your brain has created, you take actions. If your identity and goals are written in a limiting fashion, that will lead to limited actions.

❖ Actions lead to results. Limited or no actions lead to limited or no results.

❖ Results then serve as references for the brain to associate with that belief. Have you ever heard someone say, "I told you it wouldn't work" or "I knew it couldn't be done"?

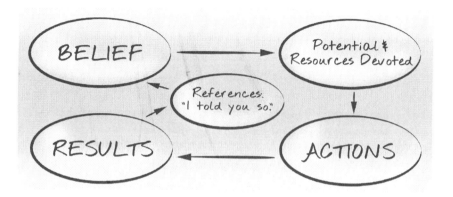

A better belief equals a positive belief. I believe I can achieve my goals, my dreams no matter how big or small. All it takes is action. Massive Action.

Massive Action means that you begin with the end in mind. Take this book for example. The massive action of writing these words is done with my vision of you reading and participating in the process of establishing your identity.

To be clear, the belief cycle is science. It is NOT a metaphor. It is not a catchy idea to help sell books. It is how the brain functions. You cannot choose whether or not you want to follow it just like you can't choose whether gravity will bring you back to Earth when you jump in the air. However, you do have a choice of what you decide to believe and how hard you will work at it. I believe in you, in your success of establishing your very powerful identity through this process. Because I believe this is a matter of fact, a matter of certainty, the massive actions required to make this book have become a natural by-product of making this a part of both my reality and yours.

When you decide what you believe, you will accomplish what ever it takes to make that belief a truth.

You MUST truly believe. When you do, you take yourself to the point of doing what ever you want. The only limitations that exist are those which you have placed upon yourself. Everything that has been accomplished, everything that has ever been done, is all by a human being. By someone just like you and me.

With that knowledge you can build upon the belief that you can accomplish anything. The belief cycle is significant in that it empowers us to accomplish what we KNOW we can. What we BELIEVE we can do.

It all starts with belief.

It won't work the other way around. It just won't. In order to make something real, you must believe that it is.

"Prove why I should believe this will work." Beginning with that attitude won't work. You must start with the belief, not proof of it.

If you truly believe you will be successful, your brain will come up with so many more ways to make it happen! If you don't believe success is an option, your brain will physically reach out to fewer areas within itself and create fewer resources. If you do believe, your brain will reach out exponentially, over and over, farther and farther. You won't limit your actions.

When you synergize each idea to achieve the goal, to reaching the belief, you take massive action. Each action creates a reference for your brain to build on and each reference will lead to ideas that reinforce the initial belief. It's a never-ending, forward moving cycle you're creating. And by creating this cycle you will achieve that end result you've had in mind.

Anything that has been done can be done better. We have the resources to improve anything that has ever been accomplished. The key is to accept the positive belief and be empowered to do what we know can be done and do it even better.

When you place limitations on yourself, you're basically locking up your brain and tossing out that key. If I were to hand you a tool or device right now, that you knew, (without me even explaining or trying to 'sell-you' on it,) would immediately make your life 10, 20, 100 times better, would you take it and use it or just put it in a closet, lock the door and throw out the key?

Do you think you might say, *"Mark, how kind of you to give this to me. This is GREAT! But really, I don't want my life to be any better so I'm just going to lock this in the closet. And since I'm never going to open this closet again, be a dear would you and toss this key in the dumpster on your way out."*

I don't think so. In fact, I think you'd take that tool and start using it immediately.

"Mark, this is GREAT! This is going to make my life so much better. Even knowing it's here and ready to use already has! Excuse me, I don't mean to be rude, but I've got to get to work with this right now!"

It's kind of like someone handing you all the money you'll ever need with no strings attached, leaving you debt free and financially secure; Not only your life time, but for generations of your family to come. Then you say, *"No thanks, I rather like having all this debt and stress in my life."*

Seems pretty ridiculous, doesn't it?

To solidify the belief in your identity, you must reinforce it. Reinforcing your identity establishes the reality of who you've decided to be. It's time to establish the certainty of who you are.

There are two simple rules to follow to reinforce your identity.

1. **Recite and Revisit it EVERY DAY, Multiple times per day for the first three weeks!**

2. **Be Passionate and play full out!**

Rule 1:
It takes approximately 21 days to replace or create a new pattern of behavior or habit. Mentally, you will run through what I call the "Change Triathlon".

❖ The first three to four days are easy. You are psyched up about the program and who you have chosen to be. Everything is new, exciting and fun!

❖ Starting around day five, you'll go through the most difficult time in the process. It will last for a week to 10 days. You'll be tempted to go back to your old patterns of thinking and behavior.

It's that need for certainty creeping in. Keep it OUT! That is not who you are anymore! Every time you're tempted, break out your identity and re-read it using the system at the end of this chapter.

❖ Finally, right around day 16 you will start to notice that you are winning the battle against the old you. Positive habits that you had to think about during the middle phase will start to become instinctual. You'll start counting down the days to the finish line and even reach beyond.

Rule 2:

When it comes to reinforcing your identity, it's not enough to just read it. You need to use your physiology, your body, to make your identity part of your DNA. When you give this process your full effort, you'll be amazed how much better you'll feel when you get through the process.

I've found using the following method works very well for most everyone:

- ❖ In a place where you can have some privacy, put on some music that makes you feel good, music that has some positive meaning for you.

- ❖ Stand up with your feet about shoulder width apart and close your eyes.

- ❖ Imagine that you have already achieved all the things you have set forth in your identity and reached all your goals. Now let yourself experience how that feels.

- ❖ When you believe that you have imagined everything you possibly could feel, jump up and yell **"YES!!!"** three times.

- ❖ Now, continue to move and begin reading your identity **OUT LOUD!!!**

- ❖ Read it three times, increasing the intensity and passion in your voice each time.

- ❖ Finish with three more **"YES!"** jumps.

Do this exercise multiple times daily for the first three weeks.

I'd like to share a few examples of how applying, and not applying Rule 2 creates an effect. Both of these examples are about women with some pretty serious health issues. These examples are of real people with whom I have worked, so... we'll call them Case Studies.

Case Study 1

This woman, we'll call her Ingrid, has fallen victim to her negativity. After running through the belief system and identity process, Ingrid continues to focus on the negative aspects of her declining health. It's easy to understand how that can happen.

When our bodies hurt and ache it makes it hard to be positive. However, as Ingrid continually fights the identity process, not fully believing, she continues to worsen in health. Ingrid has become a homebody and has a very 'woe-is-me' attitude. It's taking a very real toll not only on her but on her family and friends as well.

Let's talk about the application of what Ingrid is going through. In talking about the belief cycle, Ingrid has never fully anchored the belief that her brain can control her body. Now I want to make it clear that I'm not saying that positive thinking alone, that positivity of attitude is all that it takes to make disease go away. What it can do, is assist the body to fight the disease.

Ingrid has taken the identity process and turned it back upon itself. She's created a mirror image that shows that her identity is her illness. What has happened is that her disease has become who she is. Her disease is her identity. Do you know someone like Ingrid?

Because Ingrid is her disease, her disease continues to grow and continues to strengthen. To a certain extent, Ingrid is applying the same process you're learning here, just with a non-empowering belief or identity. She's chosen to reinforce the negativity of the disability.

The impact of this reverse sort of process application has impacted her family as well.

Ingrid's husband, a very loving and caring person, works a full time job that often requires long hours. Due to Ingrid's health, her husband still must come home, handle all the housework, and attend to her as well. And, while it's not that she can't do things like fold laundry or do dishes, by allowing her disease to be her identity she has chosen not to be active within the household.

Having formerly been a very engaging couple, Ingrid and her husband used to go out with friends and family. They'd also often entertain friends at their home. That's no longer the case. Friends and extended family still stay in touch. However, most interaction is left to phone calls and email.

Ingrid has a very real disease that is challenging to deal with. It will always be a part of her life. But instead of accepting it as only a "part" of her life, Ingrid has made it her "entire" life. She's decided to believe that her disease is who she is.

Case Study 2

This woman, let's call her Helen, also has been enduring some serious health problems. Helen has decided to believe in and embrace the identity process. She practices Rule 2 daily.

Through the certainty of her belief Helen manages her health issues by living a very full life. Enjoying family, friends, and through focusing on goals, Helen continues to thrive. In fact, she has a business of her own and stays very active within her community.

Uniquely enough, in this case Helen has endured even more severe health issues than Ingrid from Case Study 1. Helen has been through multiple surgeries and severe illnesses.

Helen truly believes in the identity process and in giving. In fact 'Giving' is part of her identity. This drives her to be very active within her community. She's one of the best at getting to know people and connecting people. She was a social networker long before Facebook or Twitter ever existed!

One of the things that cause people to gravitate to her is her openness. As people learn about her as a person, even though she doesn't put her health obstacles up front, she doesn't try to hide them either.

Through this attitude Helen teaches others that they can accomplish whatever goals they set their minds to. Helen is living the example of how the identity process truly works.

Despite severe challenges, including skeletal modifications that help her simply walk erect, Helen has decided she's able to go out and do things that those of us who are fully able bodied can do. Helen does not let what is going on within her body to detract from who she is and what she is going to accomplish.

Because health issues are sensitive and require a level of confidentiality, there isn't a lot of detail I can share in either of these case studies. However, through the simple adjustment of attitude and sincerity of belief, you can see how easy it is to improve the quality of your life through this process.

Both case studies 1 and 2 talk about health issues so it's important to make a couple things very clear:

A) A positive attitude and positive outlook do not replace the need for medical attention and proper medications.
B) Taking on and establishing a positive identity about how you're going to deal with health issues will have a positive impact.

Many case studies have shown that when people are diagnosed with cancer, their illness progresses differently based on their attitudes. Those that resign themselves to dying have shown cancers that develop more aggressively. Those who decide to live and have something to live for, often have cancers that develop slowly and many times even go into remission.

Creating a positive identity doesn't replace medicine but will have a huge impact on how well the medicine will work. You should talk about these things in depth with your doctor when discussing health issues and the power of identity. The identity you choose to defeat health issues, to overcome them, will have a huge impact on how treatments will work and you need to talk about that with your doctor.

Case Study 3

I had an opportunity to work with a high school athlete. Elizabeth is what we'll call her. She was a good athlete and a good student, but Elizabeth knew she could be better.

Elizabeth saw that her team needed stronger leadership. It was pretty unique for a high school student to recognize that need necessary to enable their success. Together we worked on visualizing what a leader does, how a leader acts and what it would take to get their team to the next level.

Elizabeth's decision to be a stronger leader was a part of her identity even before we began working with her. She just didn't realize it. She was a team player, but she wanted her team to do better, to be better, no matter what she had to do to make that happen.

Together we started working with her on the visualization process by helping her ask questions. What type of leader did her team need? What type of player did she need to be?

In athletics, especially girl's athletics, we find there are two primary types of personalities in leadership. There is either the intense 'leader by example' or the 'keeping it loose/hey relax' type of leader. A person can be both types of leader; however we usually find that they lean more one way than the other.

Within scholastic sports we also find that team or student leaders will go one way or the other usually depending on the coach. If the coach is much more of an intense type of leader, that student leader will often become more of the "Hey, come on calm down, let's concentrate but don't get too stressed out" type of leader.

So we talked about what type of coach she had and what type of leader she would need to be. We talked about how that person would think, how that person would act. What would that person do out on the floor that would help the rest of her team be better and therefore help her coach as well?

By watching her coach and understand how the players responded. She discovered that some players respond better to a pat on the back and that others responded better to a kick in the butt. She then understood that it was up to her to watch and to learn and then apply those strategies with the rest of the players on the team.

Once we helped her learn what to look for and do, she discovered that some of those things she was already doing innately, as a part of her existing identity. Once she learned what to watch for and then apply what she'd learned she was able to help her team as well as reinforce her own identity as a team leader. She was also able to apply methods to herself that helped her own growth, understanding when a pat on the back or kick in the butt most helped.

For example, when she didn't do her homework, she'd deprive herself of something she wanted. Yet, when she did get her homework done or received an A, she'd give herself some type of reward.

Through her dedication to the process I watched as a good student became a great student, a decent athlete became a great athlete. I watched as Elizabeth went from visualizing

the concept of leadership to becoming a true leader on the floor for her team. Elizabeth applied the principles and became the cornerstone of support she knew her team needed.

Three Layer Dessert Salad

Not so much a specific case study, this next example has to do with that really good three layer salad someone usually brings to summer group picnics.

You know the one: On Top there's lots of fluffy cream. It's that super sweet rich tasty layer that all the kids like to dip their fingers in.

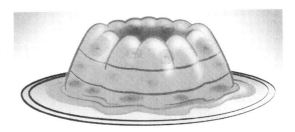

On the middle there's usually some type of Jell-O. Green, red, yellow, the color really doesn't matter. There are also usually some tasty pieces of fruit or other yummy bits mixed into the Jell-O. It's good. Not as good as the fluffy cream on top, but creates the base and ties things together well.

On the bottom there's usually some kind of lettuce or crust. And, by the end of the picnic that lettuce is wilted, the crust is soggy, it really doesn't look good. You even might find yourself wondering why on earth that was included as part of the salad that had such nice upper layers.

The thing is that salad is a lot like people and the identities they give themselves. It affects their lives well into adulthood. It affects their relationships and their careers.

Let's take a sales team for example...

That creamy fluffy layer that's so sweet you can't help but taste it first, that's the top 5% to 10% of most every sales force. They're the stars. Their identity is one of a successful sales person. They understand what it takes to succeed at their career and they do it. They do it so well that it often seems they really aren't working at it, that things just come together for them naturally.

The Jell-O layer is the 80% of most every sales force. They're good at their job. With some hard work and focused concentration they've achieved some success. They have earned a comfortable living, nice home, cars. Heck, the might even have had a few months or quarters when after lots of hard work a few deals really paid off and they became a part of that fluffy upper layer.

The people in the fluffy layer might have said, 'hey, well done and it was nice to see you here for a while, but you're not really part of our group so get back on down to your Jell-O level'. And, because that person hasn't really established and anchored their identity as one of those top level people, they shrug their shoulders and go back to where they 'belong'.

Now we're at the lettuce level, the bottom 10% of the sales team. This is usually where you find people who basically made a pretty bad career choice. They're not interested in selling, they don't see themselves as a sales person, and it's simply not a part of their true identity.

At this level, it's not necessarily that they've accepted that it's where they belong. No. Most often it's that they have no desire to become Jell-O, let alone the sweet creamy fluff of their sales team. They don't thrive and won't thrive in this role because it's not a part of their 'I AM...' statement.

The Three Layer Dessert Salad applies to any area of life. If a part of you is that rich sweet creamy fluff, it's because that is a part of your true identity. It's a part of who you've chosen to be.

Take a good hard look at what's going on within and around you. Look within your relationships with family and friends. Look within your interests and endeavors. Look within your career path, your job.

Through this process of discovering and creating your true identity you can decide what to keep, what to enhance and what you want to eliminate or change.

Frankly, I can't imagine anyone wanting to hang on to an area of their life that is like wilted lettuce or soggy tasteless crust. But then, maybe it's just about adjusting the recipe a little.

How many of you like the soft buttery crumbly crust found at the bottom of a cheese cake? Maybe you'd like to change out the wilted lettuce base for that? It's really up to you.

Maybe you don't like Jell-O and find a rich chocolaty filling more appetizing. It's OK to adjust your identity to incorporate that layer. And maybe your idea of a perfect topping is something other than cream – but whatever you like up there. It's all up to you.

The thing is, YOU have the power when developing your identity. You get to make the decisions about what stays, what changes or what goes.

Chapter 5

Share It!

"I took a deep breath and listened to the old bray of my heart. I am. I am. I am." ~ Sylvia Plath, American poet, novelist and short story writer; 1932 – 1963

There are two ways to share your identity with the world: With your words and with your actions.

1. **With your words:** Share your identity with the people you care about. Sit down with your family and tell them about the process you are going through and why you are doing it. Talk with your kids about it. Chat with your best friends about it. Discuss it with the people you work with.

    Share with them who you are becoming and the goals you have set. Share your goals with them and invite them to help you attain them.

2. **With your actions:** For the people you don't know; show them your identity by standing out in the crowd. BE the person with integrity and perseverance. BE the one who sets new standards. Hold yourself and others to those standards. BE the guiding light of character and integrity that others use to navigate through the intricate maze of life. BE a role model to yourself and others.

Now it's time to insert **Pain** and **Pleasure** into the process. Pain and pleasure are the two driving forces behind everything we do. We either want to avoid pain or gain pleasure. You're going to associate severe pain with failure and extreme pleasure with success.

You're going to celebrate every time you live up to your new identity. On the upcoming pages make a list of all the painful and pleasurable thoughts and outcomes of successes and failures you'll go through to live up to your new identity.

For example:

A painful outcome of failure to live up to your identity might be disappointing a family member or friend which in turn will make you feel bad and set you back to your old patterns keeping you from getting where you want to be.

A pleasurable outcome of continuing to live up to your identity could be knowing that you are setting the best possible example for your kids which they emulate as they grow and mature into secure and happy teens and adults.

Your kids might be excited about accomplishing new goals as they focus on traits they decide to adopt. Becoming a role model not only for themselves but for their friends as well will boost their self confidence.

Don't worry about each page being even. Over 60% of you who complete this exercise will have more negative outcomes than positive because you will do more to avoid pain than you will to gain pleasure... And that's OK.

I'd like to share a Case Study with you that emphasizes the Pain and Pleasure process.

I had an opportunity to work with an alcoholic, we'll call him Bart. Bart had been through AA. In fact he'd been through and failed the AA 12 step program several times. He was at a point in his life where the only impact, the only motivation for sincere change would come from pain.

Bart was facing the loss of his family. They were no longer going to be there for him. In fact, continuing as a drinker also meant certain death for Bart because of medical complication caused by the drinking. But even in the face of death, the thought of losing his family had more of an impact.

So, we were able to use the massive pain as a catalyst for establishing his identity as a non-drinker. Having his family there for him, not suffering the loss of those he loved ignited the motivation to decide to work with the identity process. Bart knew the pain would be too much to bear.

As he moved through the cycle of establishing the belief in his identity as a clean and sober person, Bart began to also incorporate the Pleasure portion of the process. He began to realize and see that his family still loved him very much. His parents, siblings, nieces and nephews all were very positive forces in his life.

Now, over ten years clean and sober, Bart still works with his Pain and Pleasure list on a daily basis. The process in and of itself has been incorporated into his identity of a healthy sober individual.

No matter what you, your kids, your family are dealing with in life, working the Negative and Positive Consequences lists will help you visualize what will happen as a result of establishing your identity. Take a few minutes and start your lists on the following pages. Then, review what you've listed and decide if anything needs to be added or revised.

These lists will most likely change as you continue to develop, confirm and live the identity you've chosen. That's OK. Different things will motivate us in positive and negative ways at different times of our lives. Your identity matures as you develop the ability to recognize those changes and manage your lists.

Negative Consequences

Positive Consequences

It is not enough to come up with these positive and negative consequences, keeping them only to yourself. You must share them with someone you trust to hold you accountable. Share them with someone who will hold your feet to the fire, someone who will tell you the truth: *even when it hurts.* Someone you do not want to let down or disappoint.

Also, remember to celebrate your continuing success. Be proud of your achievement of making it through another day on the right path on your journey to the life you want and deserve. Give yourself prizes or ask your loved ones to provide incentives as you continue to grow into your identity.

Together with your kids, decide how to celebrate each day as well as the incentives that will help you reach the goals you set with them. Empower your kids with keeping you in line to achieving your true identity just as much as you'll help them.

Chapter 6

Synergize It!

"The words 'I Am' are potent words; be careful what you hitch them to. The thing you're claiming has a way of reaching back and claiming you." ~ A.L. Kitselman, Industrialist, Philanthropist, Writer: 1856 – 1940

The next step to maximizing your identity and achieving your goals is to Synergize your identity.

Synergy is defined as:
"The combined effort being greater than the parts; the working together of two or more people, organizations, or things, resulting in a sum greater than that of their individual effects or capabilities."

There is an old saying, *"Birds of a feather flock together."*

In other words, people like to be around other people who are like them. This is true, but now there's a twist. We know that the vast majority of people in the world have not yet gone through the vital identity building process that you are putting in place. Since they don't yet know **WHO** they are, they "*flock*" together with people who **DO** the same things as they do. What people do and who they are being are two different things. They're related but, different.

We want to flock with other people who are BEING like us. As soon as possible, you must start networking, socializing and partnering with other like-minded people. Find those people who share your vision and goals. Work with them. Bounce ideas off each other. Push each other to greater heights. Hold each other accountable. The relationships you develop in this process can be some of the most powerful you will create in your lifetime due to the emotional attachment you have to the common goals and the achievement of them.

You should also seek out those people whose visions and goals are complimentary to yours, but different.

For example, I have a series of programs on improving selling skills and the psychology of sales. My goal is to help my clients maximize their efforts and sell more things to more people at prices higher than their competition. I have developed strategic partnerships with several banks. It's not the banks' business to train their clients how to sell more at higher prices, but it is in their best interest to do so.

If you have never done this before, it can seem like an impossible task, but it's actually very simple. Ask yourself the following questions: (**Remember the rule from Chapter 1:** *"I don't know" is an unacceptable answer. Ask yourself if you did know, what would the answer be?*)

❖ Who do I already know who shares these goals/beliefs?

❖ Who do <u>they</u> know who shares these goals/beliefs?

❖ For the people I don't know directly, who would share these goals/beliefs?

❖ Where would I find these people?

❖ What can I bring to this relationship as it develops?

❖ What can they bring to this relationship as it develops?

One of the most effective ways to accomplish synergy is to form a Mastermind Group. In the 1937 success classic titled, *Think and Grow Rich*, Napoleon Hill documented the power of Mastermind Groups to create exponential leaps in insight, wealth and success.

Simply stated, the Mastermind Group principle is that no two minds ever come together without creating a third, invisible, intangible force which is like a third mind. That "Mastermind" asks and answers questions you didn't know you needed to ask in order to solve problems and overcome challenges you didn't know you were about to face!

Dr. Napoleon Hill interviewed the wealthiest and most powerful men and women of the day in order to unlock their success secrets. And one of the most intriguing conclusions Hill came to after over 20 years of research, was ...

The most successful people in life NEVER reach the top all by themselves!

They understood the importance of collaborating with other high achievers on an on-going basis to fill, complement and supplement their knowledge gaps and make quantum leaps of insight and value creation that would have been not just difficult but impossible on their own.

In addition to old fashioned face-to-face meetings, there are a variety of ways to use technology to speed up your process. With the advent of some of the social networking technology and websites, you can expand your reach across the globe in a short period of time.

Below are just a few tools you can use to search out and connect with like minded souls as well as from instant groups or networks:

www.facebook.com
Facebook is a social networking site that enables you to communicate on-line with family and friends. Through use of associated applications, it also enables you to meet new people online when you share and compare interests.

www.twitter.com
With Twitter you connect with others by following their information feed and others follow you as well. Often thought of as a micro blog, Twitter is actually a communication tool with publicly time-lined real-time conversations.

www.youtube.com
YouTube is unique in that it is both a video based social networking site as well as the world's largest video search engine. Through the visual medium of video you can create your own channel, produce and upload videos with nearly any range of content from purely amateur to professionally edited content and engage others in an interactive 24 hour a day 365 day a year conversational format.

www.linkedin.com
LinkedIn is a business oriented professional networking site. It's often been described as 'Facebook for Professionals'. In its most basic form the profile section is like creating your resume on-line. Beyond that there are groups you can join enabling you to connect with other professionals and continually build your professional network.

www.plaxo.com
Plaxo sets itself apart by being a socially networked address book. It tracks other social networking sites and integrates information from additional accounts so that you're updated through one resource.

www.myspace.com
In the last quarter of 2010 MySpace changed its format from a general networking resource to become focused on the music industry. It no longer competes with Facebook as a general social networking site, and targets younger users with a particular interest in music. It's a great resource for budding bands and other musical artists.

Because there are so many people using a variety of different social networking sites to connect, you might consider selecting two or three to try, if you're not already using them. Integrating the use of a few different social networking resources will enable you to communicate with family, friends as well as meet new and interesting people.

Chapter 7

Be It!

"Renew thyself completely each day; do it again, and again, and forever again." ~ Cited by Thoreau in Walden; a Chinese inscription.

Lastly, you have to become your identity. This process is designed to help you embed your identity into the core of your being. It's not enough to read this book, either alone or with your kids, and write down some things on a piece of paper. It's not enough just to want it.

You've got to become it!

Some of you, like me, have been taught the "Do-Have-Be" model for how to be successful in business and in life. If you're not familiar with it, it goes a little something like this:

Do – We've been conditioned that we have to "do" things to be successful. The more we "do" the more money we will make. When a crisis hits, everyone asks what should be "done" about it. We can't just "do" nothing. For heavens sake, somebody "do" something!

In pop culture, Nike built an extremely successful marketing campaign around the slogan, "Just Do It". It gave everyday Joe's the idea that they too could be like their idols who use Nike products.

Have – If we "do" enough, then we will "have" something. Maybe it's respect, money, adulation, praise, love, whatever. Many people measure who they are by what they have or don't have.

They need to have a bigger house or newer car than the next guy. They need to have a certain level of respect or appreciation. In their subconscious mind, they have set a parameter that once they have a certain level or amount of something (it could be anything), that then they will finally be... _____! [*Fill in the blank*]

Be – In this model, once you "have" enough of that "thing" you will finally BE something. You can be rich, respected, admired, loved, secure, etc.

Would you agree that this is the model we've all been taught to follow in order to achieve success? Is it really that simple? If you just go out and "do" stuff, then you can have everything you've ever wanted?

If that's true, then why doesn't everyone "do" it?

Want the answer? Do you? Really? Then turn the page.

BECAUSE IT'S WRONG!!

The model we've been taught as the foolproof way to achieve success is backwards. As you learned earlier in this book, who you are being everyday determines what it is you will or will not do. Here is how it really works:

BE – Be the person you have outlined in this book. Live up to your new and true identity. Don't be embarrassed because you have taken a step that most haven't even thought of or don't have the guts to do.

Embrace your greatness! Let it emanate from you like energy from the sun. Watch as other great people, things and opportunities start to gravitate toward you and orbit around you.

DO – As we discussed in Chapter 4, what we "do" is dependent upon what we believe and the conviction with which we believe it. If you "did" things half-assed with little forethought or planning, then you should not be surprised when you get the same results as other people who "do" things the same way.

Now that you are armed with this knowledge you can use your past as a learning experience. Do things differently. Sure there are going to be situations where you're not sure what to do. Maybe you've only known one way to react to something and you're still in the process of changing that old pattern. (*If this is the first time you're reading this book, that's where you're at.*)

If you're not sure how to do things differently, refer back to Chapter 1 and ask those people who you admire and who have achieved what you want. If you can't reach them, then ask yourself what would they do in this situation and is it congruent with my identity?

If all else fails and you need to make a split second decision as to what to do about something you've encountered in the past and gotten non-desirable results, I recommend the Costanza Strategy.

The Costanza Strategy is based on the character George Costanza from the hit TV show, Seinfeld. Simply stated, it is to do the opposite of what you have done in the past.

Let me make one thing VERY CLEAR. The Costanza Strategy is not a substitute for research and hard work. It is ONLY to be used when there is no other option due to time and circumstances.

Have – Each and every one of us has what we have because of who we are being. We all have exactly what we have earned and what we deserve. This may seem harsh, but it is true. I know because I've been there.

This is not to say that you are not a good person if you have not achieved your goals or a certain level of success. Quite the contrary, you've been doing your best with the tools you had at your disposal. You deserve so much more than what you have so far.

Now you have a proven system to get you there and support mechanisms in place to assist you along the way.

All successful people have goals.

Your first assignment for this chapter is to write down three detailed goals. The next three pages are goal worksheets my team and I developed to help you with this process. Be extremely precise in the wording of your goals. Give yourself a finish line and benchmarks along the way so you can measure your progress.

Google your brain.

Our brains work through a series of instantaneous electrical connections. I'm not talking about a static-shock sort of spark, like when you rub your feet across the carpet. It's not like that.

What happens between the electric synapses is that a bit of the electricity is left behind and creates a physical connection between parts of the brain. It becomes sort of like an electronic spider web. The more those sections of the brain connect, the stronger the web.

When it comes to human behavior the key is to access the different parts of the brain that are interconnected by these webs. Because of these webs we can literally program our brain. Our brain is like a computer. Or, actually, computers are like our brains.

The best analogy for today's kids comes from analyzing how computers reflect how we think. To access our internal information we ask ourselves questions. When we don't like the answer we receive, we need to ask ourselves better questions.

The human brain is an amazing thing. It has stored everything you have ever experienced, seen, heard, smelled or felt. And, each of these "files" is stored in a different area of your brain. Retrieving or recalling each different type of "file" requires a different physical process. Why are some of those things easier to access or recall than others?

Well, we all have a preferred mode of communication and comprehension. Each of us falls into one of three main categories: See-ers, Hear-ers, and Feel-ers. For example, I am a See-er. I can watch someone do something and learn it quickly. If you were to "tell" me how to do something, it would take multiple times for me to get it right.

Which is your preferred mode? What about your kids? If you're not sure what your (or your kids) preferred mode is, your language will let you know. See-ers use words as if they were describing a picture – size, color, clarity, brightness, perspective, etc. "Do you 'see' what I'm saying?" Hear-ers use words that are related to the ear and/or sounds like "sounds good to me" or "her face rings a bell." Feel-ers use words about feelings or actions. "I'm not comfortable moving forward" or "I need to get a handle on this."

What it comes down to is, our brain is the internet full of the information and resources we desire and the process of thought is our search engine. So when we think, we're Google-ing our brain.

There's an old saying in the computer programming world: Garbage In/Garbage Out. It means we're only going to get the same quality out as what we put in. Understanding this enables us to improve the quality of our thought process.

So, now that you understand that different types of files are accessed differently from different parts of our brains that can help us Search Engine Optimization or SEO. If you are a see-er, you'll access the video or picture sites in your brain more often. Your brain recognizes that and starts to predict you will want to continue to come back often. Through the physical connections in the brain, it will do the equivalent of bookmarking those areas of the brain for quick and easy access. Likewise, if you are a hear-er or feeler, your brain will set up the preferred links with those parts of the brain... and so on.

The better questions we Google our brains with, the better the answers will be that we give ourselves. By improving the questions we ask ourselves, we improve the identity we're creating.

There is a Recipe for results. It has six ingredients or, steps. You must follow each step carefully. It's a complete process.

The Six 'R's of Success

1 ~ Results: Know Your Outcome
2 ~ Reason: Know the Reason, or, Know Your 'Why'
3 ~ Road M.A.P.: Make a **M**assive **A**ction **P**lan
4 ~ Recognize: Recognize the Results from Your MAP
5 ~ Revise: Change the Plan As Needed Based On Results
6 ~ Rejoice: Celebrate Your Achievement

To help you understand this a little better I'll take you through the...

Six 'R' Process

1st Results ~ Know Your Outcome

Know what your goals are going to look like once they're achieved. You have to know what you're going for. Whether you're achieving a goal, or getting into a relationship, you have to know what it will be like when you've hit that goal.

We used to use an old saying, *"Write the press release and work the deal backwards from there."* You have to know what you're aiming for. And, you have to know this, not in just general information, but in every detail.

You need to know what it will look like, sound like, feel like, taste like, what it will smell like. Think about what you want your outcome to be in very specific terms. Be aware of every detail.

You have to know it, own it. It has to be part of you.

When we're talking about this I AM process you have to act 'as-if', knowing the identity you want and acting as if you are who you want to be.

2nd Reason ~ Know the Reason for Your Outcome, or… Know Your 'Why'

Why is this important you? Why is this important to the people on your team, your family, friends, your spouse, and your children?   You need to know your 'why' because these things apply to every aspect of your life.

This is not about just being 'successful' or 'rich.' Those are very vague terms. You have to know why this is so important by understanding every intricate detail. This has to become a part of your DNA, a part of _who you are_.

This has to be so much a part of you because if you don't have a good enough, a detailed enough reason 'why'; you're not going to be able to use all the resources at your disposal to make this happen.

3rd Road M.A.P. ~ Bridge the Gap in the Road

Massive **A**ction **P**lan means that nothing is going to stop you. You will go and do whatever you have to do to make 'this' happen.

Now I've heard people say, *"Well I've tried everything…"*

Yet, when you really get down to details and question them, down to the nuts and bolts of things… You ask how many things they've tried, how many ideas they've had, you discover that they've tried three, four, maybe five at the most. As opposed to saying, *"OK, that didn't work"* and going out and trying something different.

People are much more likely to bridge that gap, to do something, when they first have that idea. At that moment, you're ready. You don't want to build a little bridge. You don't want it to be weak. You want to build a bridge of concrete and steel. You can do this by scheduling the first thing you want to do.

Now I realize that certain ideas you may have aren't the kind that you can just go 'jump off a cliff' and make it happen. There's planning that needs to be done, especially if you want to do things properly.

Start right there. Make a big plan. The plan is the first piece of your bridge. Don't just make a little plan to try for a little bit of success. Make a Concrete Plan for Massive Success!

Now the key is it's not enough to just have great ideas. For every great thing that's been invented that has made life easier for mankind, there have been equally as many that have been thought up and been put on a back-burner never to be seen again.

So...

Where would we be as a country, as an economic society, without others bridging the gaps that appear? Who's to say where we'd be as a people, as human beings on this Earth, if everyone had bridged gaps for themselves with some of their ideas that have happened in the past?

What if everybody put this type of approach into play instead of saying, "*Ahhh... I could never do this. I'm just a* _____."?

4th Recognize ~ Recognize Your Results
You're going to discover that not every idea is in its perfect form when it is thought of. You have to recognize the results you're getting from your actions.

Sometimes people will say, "*We've done things in this industry this way for 10, 20, 50... 100 years.*"

There's also the old saying, "*If it's not broke don't fix it.*"

But, just because something's been done a certain way doesn't mean it can't be improved upon. It doesn't mean new things shouldn't be tried just because everything's working at a reasonable rate. To evaluate improvements and modifications, you need to recognize the results you're getting back from the world.

For example; if you're a salesperson and you want to try a new way of selling or marketing your product or service you want to be able to recognize those results. You want to be able to see, to measure. Am I doing the same, better? Or, am I doing worse?

If you're doing worse, you may want to take a look at tweaking what you're doing. Take a look at your plan and determine if you're far enough into your plan that what you're seeing is measurable. Is what you're seeing relevant to your plan?

Part of recognizing your results is going back to the planning stages of your massive action. You have to build tracking methods into your plan. It can't just be a 'feeling' of how you're doing. You have to be able to quantify, measure, how you're doing so your results become visible.

This becomes the basis of "*How will I measure a success?*" Or, "*How will I adjust and modify my plan to stay on track and achieve my goal?*"

5th Revise ~ Modify Your Approach... As Needed

If your idea has given you the results you were looking for, you may not need to modify your approach. However, if you're not getting the results you are looking for, like you were expecting an increase but getting a decrease, then you need to take a look at why that is.

It's time to change what you're doing. Make sure that change is measurable so you know you're on the right track and you're maintaining and building on the momentum from previous changes.

The key is if something isn't working you need to fix it. Don't keep doing the same thing over and over again getting the same results if those results are not what you need them to be. **That's just stupid!**

6th Rejoice ~ Celebrate Your Success
This may be the most important step.

If you've been successful...

If you've taken things where you want to take them...

If you've gone where you want to go...

If you've done what you want to do...

CELEBRATE THAT SUCCESS!

Enjoy your success. Share it with the rest of the world. There is no reason why you should stay where you are in life if you're not that same person any more. Celebrate! Have a party!

Now, it's time to start putting your recipe together. Begin by writing down some goals on the next few pages. State your goal as if it has already happened. Remember, you're starting by knowing your outcome.

For each goal include steps 1 through 6. These won't look perfect the first time you put them down. That's OK. This is only the beginning, your starting point. You'll be refining them as you move ahead.

Now go grab a pen or pencil and have some fun!

Goal #1

Goal #2

Goal #3

Now compare your goals against the outline of your identity. Are they congruent? Do they feel like they go together? Does your identity need to be stronger? Do your goals need to be more robust?

If so then…

If not then…

With goals and identity matching, now…

Maintain the momentum you've started here with me time/my time. Sit down and think for yourself with a pad of paper and pen in hand. Write solutions to issues. Answer the questions of 'how should I act?', 'what should I do?' Always evolve and move forward as you do these exercises every day.

Revisit this maintenance process every single day. Stay associated with practicing your identity. Read the book again and teach someone else how to do this. Teach your kids, teach your family members.

Notice the difference you will feel. See how you are acting differently when things are not congruent with the identity you've chosen for yourself. You'll discover that when you're not in sync with your identity, you'll be able to tell and adjust.

The 10 Secrets to Empower Kids
& Awaken the Child Within You

Secret #1: Be Great!

Whether an elementary school student or a corporate CEO, how a person finishes the statement, 'I AM...' defines who they are, their beliefs about themselves, their world, and the standards they live by. How they finish that statement is their identity.

It is the driving force behind the behaviors exhibited both in public and in private. Psychologists and Psychiatrists will tell you that it is nearly impossible for a person to consistently act in a fashion that is not congruent with his or her identity. So the question is, how do we get our kids to have identities that empower them rather than hinder them as they grow?

Kids are born as blank slates. They don't have all the self-doubt, self-pity, and other negative BS (*Belief Systems*) that many adults demonstrate on a regular basis. If they were born with those negative traits, most children would never walk, speak, or feed themselves. They would give up after a handful of failed attempts. In their minds, kids were born to be successful. They adapt. They overcome. They persevere.

So, what happens as kids grow up? How do self-doubt and negative beliefs creep in? There is an old saying, *"People will live up to, or down to, your expectations."* That is only partially true. The truth is that people will live up to THEIR OWN expectations.

The problem is most people, children and adults alike, have never given conscious thought to what they expect from themselves. That being the case, how do kids know what to expect from themselves? They learn from the people around them, mostly their parents, older siblings, and teachers. As a parent or adult role model, it is imperative that you discuss and demonstrate what you expect from your kids and what they should expect from themselves.

This brings us to Secret #1 for Empowering Kids – BE GREAT!

In my house, we have a ritual every time we say Good Bye to each of our children as they are leaving for school, a sporting event, or just to go out. I'm sure you have a similar ritual. You kiss them. You hug them. You tell them you love them. With excitement and enthusiasm, the last thing we say to them is "BE GREAT!" To which, they reply with matching vigor, "I AM!"

It seems like a little thing, and it is. Just like a single brick is a little thing. But when combined with other tools and materials (*like the other nine secrets for empowering kids*), each brick provides the foundation upon which an empowering belief system is built. It takes time to create habits and thought patterns.

According to different experts, it can range from days to weeks. I've found about 21 days to be the norm for creating lasting effects. Multiple times each day your child needs to be reminded that he or she is GREAT. Their verbal and physical response then anchors the same affirmation in their subconscious mind. Over time, the connections between different parts of their brain grow to be so strong that BEING GREAT literally becomes part of their brain chemistry.

This is not about driving your kids or being a *"Tiger Mom."* This is about giving your kids the tools and guidance to decide for themselves. It's not about self-esteem. It's not about feeling good about trying and failing. It's about success! It's about kids having the confidence to try and the perseverance to keep going. Your kids will surprise you by being the person they know they can be when you believe in them.

Tell your kids to Be GREAT. Be OUTSTANDING. Be whatever your POWER word is. To which their response is, 'I AM'. You will be amazed by their growth over a relatively short period of time.

Secret #2: Make Fear Fun!

According to the Encarta Dictionary, fear is defined as "an unpleasant feeling of anxiety or apprehension caused by the presence or anticipation of danger." The most commonly use synonyms are panic, anxiety, and worry. How often do we hear those words in the media these days?

The key words in that definition are the "*presence*" or "*anticipation*." There are different types of fear that people feel. Some are instinctive and helpful while others are invented in the mind and hurtful.

The instinctive fears show up in the "***presence***" of danger. It is your fight or flight response. These fears require little or no conscious thought. The instinctive part of our brain takes over and reacts for us.

It is the "***anticipation***" that is the problem with so many kids (*and adults*) in our society. Several studies and surveys have been conducted over the years ranking the Top 10 Strongest or Most Common Fears. The fear of public speaking is always ranked number one or two, yet the fear of death is always in the middle of the pack. Does that make any sense to you?

Here is Secret #2 for Empowering Kids – Make Fear Fun!

Change the association of fear in the minds of your kids and yourself. When you and your kids confront the things you are fearful of and overcome them, the power of your identity grows. When you attack something that you were afraid of and discover, *"that's it? That's what I was afraid of?"* it's incredibly empowering.

Before you read on, let me make clear the distinction between Fear and Risk. I am NOT advocating for you and your family to seek out risky activities as a means of empowering yourselves. Let's use a common activity that millions of people engage in every day as an example: flying on an airplane.

Fear of flying is consistently ranked at or near the top of the most common fears of people in the U.S.A. Yet, flying is statistically proven to be the safest mode of transportation. So, why are so many people afraid to fly? It is the *"anticipation."*

Earl Nightingale was a prodigious speaker and author in his day. His publishing company, Nightingale Conant, is still one of the largest publishers in the field of personal and professional development. Mr. Nightingale conducted a study on the subject of what people worry about. Below are his results:

* **Things that never happen: 40%**. That means 40 percent of the things you worry about will never occur anyway.

* **Things over and past that can't be changed: 30%.** In other words, these things can't be changed by all the worry in the world.

* **Needless worries about our health: 12%.** These are *'what if...'* worries. If you have no history of a disease in your family, why fear it?

* **Petty, miscellaneous worries: 10%**. These are the worries like, *"Did I leave the garage light on..."* Or, *"Did I vacuum under the sofa..."*

* **Real, legitimate worries: 8%.** Only 8 percent of your worries are worth concerning yourself about. 92% of our worries have no substance at all!

Human beings are creatures of habit. Generally speaking, we don't like to change those habits, those behavior patterns. I have found that most people fear change, they fear the unknown. Their fear is there even if that change promises to be for the better.

Kids fear changes like moving to a new neighborhood, going to a new school, making new friends, or trying something they wouldn't simply because they think they won't be good enough at it. So, how do we help our kids to challenge themselves and confront these types of invented fears? We help them by having them ask themselves questions like:

If I know I will succeed, what would I do first?
What will happen if I do....?
What will happen if I don't...?

Helping them ask these questions is a simple and important step. These questions change the brain's focus. No longer is your child focused on the fear which leads to continual reinforcement of the fear. The focus is now on the positive outcome. Now the brain is looking for resources to make that positive outcome a reality rather than focusing on the fear that prevented action from being taken.

We have just changed the association in the mind of your child related to that fear. Now they will feel challenged and empowered rather than afraid and anxious. As this is repeated over time, it will create new empowering habits and behavior patterns, while boosting their Belief System.

One of my own personal mantras is, *"If I can't then I must."* If there is something I think is preventing me from reaching my desired outcome or goal, then I must do it. Facing my own fears becomes a challenge, a game of sorts. But by using this secret on myself, I have rigged the game. I win every time simply by confronting the fear and overcoming it.

For example, I tried bungee jumping because of my former fear of heights. Now, participating in extreme sports isn't part of my identity. I don't go bungee jumping every day, but it was related to one of my fears that I felt I needed to face and overcome.

Stand up to your fears. Don't let fear hold you or your kids back from the success you are destined for. To quote a good friend of mine, Sarah Victory, challenge yourself and your kids to *"do something brave every day."*

Secret #3: No Means Yes.

By nature, people like be right. We like to be correct. It makes us feel smarter. Kids are people. They like to be right too. Think back to FEAR as addressed in Secret #2. If a kid is afraid to look or sound dumb or un-cool if he or she does something incorrectly, how likely do you think that child is to participate in class, join a club or sport, or try new things?

No Means Yes is about framing the choices your kids have so that either choice is correct or a positive outcome.

Welcome to Secret #3 for Empowering Kids – No Means Yes.

Has your child ever said something like the following statement to you? *"I know what you're going to say so I'm not even going to ask."* If so, in return you should say, *"Well, either way you're going to be right then. So, if you ask and I do say no then that means you were smart enough to think ahead and know what the answer was. And if my answer is yes, then you get to do what it is you really want to do anyway. So… either way you wind up winning, you come out ahead!"*

What this means is that with our kids, (*and even ourselves really*), we need them to frame their questions so that no means yes. Either way, we've created a successful outcome.

This empowerment secret is also useful in the classroom. Many of the teachers I work with use the story of Thomas Edison to demonstrate this to their students.

Legend has it that Thomas Edison was being interviewed by a newspaper reporter about his many incredible inventions. The reporter began asking questions focusing on the numerous failed experiments while working on inventing the electric light bulb. According to Edison's own journals, there were over 2,000 experiments that did NOT produce a viable light bulb. The reporter asked how Edison could keep going after failing so many times.

Edison's reply was a perfect example of No Means Yes. He said, "*I didn't fail over 2,000 times. I succeeded in eliminating over 2,000 possibilities. I was not discouraged, because every wrong attempt discarded is another step forward.*"

Each of The 10 Secrets to Empower Kids are helpful and important it its own right. Like building materials at a construction site that make a tall skyscraper, the 10 Secrets combine to build an identity and belief system that reaches for new heights. However, Secret #3 has added importance in that it connects several other secrets with each other. It serves to spread the weight across the entire system. It keeps kids thinking positively when circumstances might normally dictate otherwise.

When practiced on a regular basis with kids, No Means Yes teaches kids to use the same strategy for themselves. Now, not only will they ask more questions, but they will also begin coming up with their own creative solutions. And that is when the magic happens.

By turning no into yes we give our kids the ability to examine the choices that are presented to them and weigh the outcomes. Ultimately, by understanding the outcome in advance, your kids are able to plan their actions with more forethought, thereby, making better choices.

How can you start to employ No Means Yes with your kids and just as importantly with yourself? Read Secret #4.

Secret #4: Set The Example.

How many times have you seen one of your own "*less than favorable*" behaviors exhibited by one or more of your kids? It could be something as small as using poor table manners or as significant as lashing out in anger when things don't go their way. Either way, it is vital for you to understand that children learn how to react from the people in their environment. They mimic the behaviors of their role models. Simply stated, kids emulate adults behaviors until they become anchored and then those behaviors become their own.

If you are reading this, then you obviously want your kids to be empowered and successful. If you want your kids to be more empowered, YOU need to be more empowered. Set the example!

You have to put-up or shut-up with Secret #4 – Set the Example.

If you want your kids to act in a moral or acceptable way, you have to take the lead. If you don't want your kids to steal, then you shouldn't. If you don't want them to smoke, then you can't smoke. If you want them to be drug free, you must be as well. You have set the example.

Things are very cut and dried with kids. This is a key thing to remember when dealing with children, especially with younger kids. Something either "*Is*" or it "*Is Not.*"
Like many behaviors, justification is something they learn from adults as they get older. Let me share a story with you that I witnessed first hand...

A man was with his young son in the local bakery. As part of their trip to the bakery, dad was incorporating math into their journey. He asked his son how much a particular item cost. Then he asked how much three of those would cost... and so on.

On this day, it was very busy at the bakery. When their number was called, the dad and son placed their order and paid in cash. When the girl behind the counter gave him his change, she mistakenly gave him ten dollars too much. The son noticed and started to say something. The father made a motion to the boy by putting his hand up with one finger extended, the international signal for "*hold on a minute.*"
He took his change, put it in his pocket, and walked toward the door. The boy had a look of confusion on his face.
By the look on that boy's face I guessed his dad had told him that it is not acceptable to steal to take something that doesn't rightfully belong to you. Yet, that's what the boy just witnessed. What did this boy just learn? Has something like this ever happened to you?

Most people (*and therefore kids*), are visual learners. Watching you is how they learn what is acceptable in society and what is not. This is why in certain places around the country one set of behaviors might be normal, but in other areas, those same behaviors are completely unacceptable.

Kids learn that by watching what goes on around them. They learn by watching adults in their environment. What we're doing with Secret #4, by setting the example, is teaching our kids that they can become their own role models. They'll begin setting the example for kids younger than them.

They might even begin to get adults on board by making their behaviors visible.

There is an old saying, *"Actions speak louder than words."* While this may seem harsh to some of you reading this, what I am about to say may be the most important thing in this book. If you don't lead by example, your words to your child are EMPTY.

They hear you say one thing and see you doing another. While they may be too young to have a vocabulary word for it, kids recognize the hypocrisy. Everyone, regardless of age, wants to know that they can trust the people who are closest to them.

If a person's words and actions are incongruent, a shadow of doubt is placed in the mind of the recipient. Can I really trust what this person says? Do you want your kids thinking this about you? And, as they get older, they will find someone (*or a group of people like a gang*) whose actions and words are congruent with each other – either positive or negative. Wouldn't you rather be the trusted source for your kids?

POSITIVE OUTCOME

NEGATIVE OUTCOME

Secret #5: Decisions have Consequences.

Few things empower people more (*especially kids*) than giving them ownership of the decisions that effect their lives and circumstances. When they decide for themselves, they have both emotional and intellectual '*skin*' in the game.

Let your kids make choices for themselves and then let them live with results, be they positive or negative. Kids must understand how the decisions they make affect their lives. To be clear, I'm not saying that you turn total control of your seven-year-old's entire life over to him or her. As the parent, you have the power and the responsibility to use it wisely.

Going back to Secret #3, how you help your children frame their choices goes a long way toward them making good choices, creating empowering routines. For example, if your child is focused on getting an "A" in a given subject, what choice do you think he/she would make the night before a test: study or play video games?

Today, too many children are inadvertently being taught that decisions don't have consequences. Well meaning parents and teachers will react by saying... "*Oh, well, he's just a kid.*" As such, the kids think that particular behavior is OK since they didn't get in trouble. They can do what they want and nothing bad will happen. If that is the <u>consistent</u> response from the adults in their life, what else are they supposed to think?

Faced with a choice? Use Secret #5 – Decisions Have Consequences.

We all want the best for our kids and to protect them from pain. Many parents act as a shield that keeps any and all '*bad*' things from their child. In reality, as parents we should be more like a filter than a shield.

Some things should be let through so that the kids can learn for themselves. Think about it. Of the life lessons you have learned in your lifetime, which ones were most impactful? What you were told by someone else or what you experienced for yourself?

Let me tell you a story that demonstrates the simple process of Secret #5...

As we all know, doing homework is a vital part of excelling in school. In our house, we have agreed that homework is done before any entertainment such as watching TV, playing a video game, or hanging out with friends. As concerned parents, we ask questions about the homework:
Do you understand it?
Is it done?
Is it put away in the correct folder?
Is it ready for school tomorrow?
The answers all come back yes, yes, and yes.

Over the years, at one time or another each one of my kids has forgotten their finished homework at home. That's understandable. Everyone makes a mistake once in a while. Sometimes life breaks up our normal routine and we get distracted. It happens.

Helping them realize that their Decisions Have Consequences isn't some kind of zero tolerance policy. It is about teaching kids how to be responsible for their actions.

The first time forgetting their homework happens, I help them out. I called the school and talked to the teachers. I've hand delivered, emailed or faxed homework. That night, I talked with the child who forgot his/her homework and tell them that I helped out. I also explain to them that this is the only time I will do that for them. It is up to them to learn from the experience and make sure it doesn't happen again.

It's up to you to decide how you want to work with your kids. My philosophy is to assist the first time in conjunction with a discussion about the consequences of a repeat offense. Then, if it happens again, they have to deal with the consequences. It is then up to me to be <u>consistent</u> and live up to my word. This may be difficult for some of you initially, but I assure you it will pay off in the long run.

Secret #6: Be Consistent.

Whether you realize it or not, the simple strategy of being consistent fills multiple needs for your child's development. There are some things that EVERY child should get consistently no matter what.

Every child should know that he/she is loved unconditionally every second of every day. As a parent, there is NOTHING more important than that. Being loved is the most secure feeling that anyone, child or adult, can have. That being a given, let's explore some more benefits of being consistent with your kids.

When it comes to parenting, one of the most important things is Secret #6 – Be Consistent.

As discussed earlier, the number one psychological need for any human being is the feeling of Certainty. Certainty is what allows us to feel secure in our own knowledge and our lives. There are things we know that will have a predictable outcome like the lights coming on when we flip the light switch or the car speeding up when pressing the gas pedal and stopping when pressing the brake. These are truths that we adults have learned over our many years of life experience.

Think back to the last time flipped the light switch while walking into a room and the lights did NOT go on. Didn't you momentarily stop in your tracks? Temporarily, your world was shaken as you searched for answer to the first question that popped into your head... What the _____?

You have to remember, kids do not have the benefit of our life history. They are experiencing many things for the first time. That's why they ask so many "*why*" questions. Why does this happen? Why did that happen? Why is the sky blue? You know what I'm talking about.

The reason they ask so many questions is that they are looking for information to fill in the gaps in their perception. They have no references to look back at to explain "*why*" something happened. They have no other option than to go their most trusted source, you!

If you want your kids to be empowered, it is vital to their development that you have a strong empowering identity. It is equally as important that you consistently maintain high standards for yourself and your children. It provides them the certainty they need. With that certainty they can just do what kids naturally do best – learn and grow.

Consistency is what keeps everything going; it's what forms the patterns that enable a person's identity to become bigger, stronger, and more powerful.

It is important to remember is that Consistency is a double-edged sword. It's just as easy to become consistent with behavior that supports bad habits as it is with behavior that is positive. I'll use myself as an example.

When I was younger I was a world class athlete. After an injury derailed my chances at professional career and I grew into adulthood, it became easy to get out of the routine of working out, going to the gym, and staying at my peak physical condition. Those bad habits were a consistent behavior.

Seemingly overnight, I'd notice my pants getting too tight. I'd remind myself that changing my behavior would help me stay in shape. It gave me an opportunity to re-adjust and reinforce consistent positive behavior patterns.

I do want to make this point clear:
Being consistent does not mean you should be completely inflexible. These secrets are not about creating a policy and procedure manual for raising kids. It's about raising the happiest and most well adjusted kids possible while enjoying the journey together with our kids. The art of parenting is knowing how to make the flexibility the exception rather than the rule.

Secret #7: Let Your Kids Think.

You don't want to teach your kids **what** to think. You want to teach them **how** to think. The process of thinking is actually the process of asking questions. Questions do two things:
1) Questions stimulate responses.
2) Questions guide the focus of whoever is involved in those questions.
If you're not getting good answers (*or any answers at all*), ask different and better questions.

How many times have your kids asked you a question from their homework? How many times have your kids asked you what to do in a particular situation? How many times have you told them the answer?

The key to Secret #7 to Empower Kids is to Let Your Kids Think for themselves.

The way to do this is, when kids ask you a question; help them by responding with a question that stimulates them to find the answer rather than just telling them the answer. In other words, ask them a question about their question. Remember, the person who asks the questions controls the focus of the conversation. This focuses the child on finding his or her own answer to the problem rather than focusing on you for the answer.

Another way to do this is asking kids, "*What do you think?*" Most commonly you get the response, "*Idunah*" which is Kid-speak for "I don't know." When you pose the "*What do you think?*" question you will find that one of two things happen.

The way the brain works, it takes that phrase, "*I don't know*" as the statement it is. It takes it as a command. This gives the brain permission to shut down and, not know. Instead of going back and looking into that vast storage vault of information our brains have, it simply accepts the command not to know. Your brain doesn't even bother to go look for the answer on that subject.

The best response to "*I don't know*" is to say "*I'm not asking you what you know. I'm asking you what you think.*" Explain to your child how they can never be wrong in what they think. A fact can be wrong, but what you think can't be. The response might not be the correct answer to their question, but it is the correct answer to what they think. Remember Secret #3: No Means Yes.

If your child still says he or she does not know what she thinks, one of two things is happening. Either he or she really is being lazy and doesn't want to be bothered or he/she really doesn't have a thought. If that's the case, what is the best way to stimulate thought? Ask another question!

We don't want the kids' brains to shut down. That means, "*I don't know*" is NEVER an acceptable answer. If they still respond that way, it is time to break out the master key to unlock the brain. When they say, "*I don't know,*" redirect them by saying, "*I know you don't know and that's OK. But, if you did know what would the answer be?*"

What that does is reframe the question. You'll be amazed at the answers, often correct, when you enable their brains to look for the information they already have. This is because the questions focus the thought.

The final tool to use with your kids dealing with problem solving is having them ask themselves what they DO know about a particular problem. This takes the focus off of what they don't know and allows them to make progress.

Better questions make for better answers.

Secret #8: Your Kids are NOT Mini-Me!

Even if they look just like you, every child is unique in his or her own way.

Just because you enjoy baseball, dancing, music or reading, doesn't mean your kids will enjoy the same things. Just because you have a skill or affinity for something doesn't mean that they will. Just because you are in the same gene pool doesn't mean your kids swim in it using the same stroke.

Not just a 'Chip-Off-The-Old-Block', Secret #8 – Your Kids Are Not Mini-Me.

Encourage your kids to try different things and follow their passions. Let them find out for themselves what they enjoy. If it happens that you share some of the same interests, fantastic! You'll have something you can share together for the rest of your lives. You can provide guidance and advice as they move along on life's journeys.

What happens if your kids discover that they like things that are different than your interests? What will you do? Will you tell them they can't do those things? Did your parents do that to you? How did that work?

You might want to look into what your kids like. Ask them what makes it so intriguing to them. Why do they like it so much? This way you can help them along their discovery path as well as share conversations with them about their learning process.

Helping them through their discovery process enables you to learn how they see things differently from you. Treat them as an individual. Ask them questions. Talk with your kids. They want to share with you.

As they grow, your kids will search out like minded people; people with similar interests. Take this opportunity to learn more about their interests even if they're different from yours so you can help them develop and continue to be a strong part of their lives.

There are parents out there (*we've all seen them*), who want their kids to do all the things they never did. Unfortunately, we've all also seen the kid who is miserable just trying to make their parents happy. Parenting is not raising your kids to be just like you... or, a better version of you. It is about providing your kids with the love, guidance, and encouragement to be the best and happiest version of them.

There is a story that is attributed to the late John Lennon. It goes something like this...

John said, "*When I was 5 years old, my mother always told me that happiness was the key to life. When I went to school, they asked me what I wanted to be when I grew up. I wrote down 'happy'. They told me I didn't understand the assignment, and I told them they didn't understand life.*"

Isn't that the kind of wisdom we really want our kids to have?

Secret #9: Talk *WITH* Your Kids, Not *TO* Your Kids.

Too many adults today talk to their kids and not with their kids. They are constantly *'telling'* them what to do and how to think. From the time babies are able to move around their home, they are barraged with negative reinforcement. *"No, no baby. Don't touch that. Don't eat that. Don't pull Fido's ears."* Sound familiar?

Infants and toddlers need constant supervision. Until they can communicate with us grown-ups, we have few other options to keep them safe.

Watching kids grow up is one of the true gifts and wonders of the world. You laugh together and cry together. Your bond grows stronger every day. What could possibly go wrong? This is where the parenting-disconnect between kids and adults happens. Over time that disconnect is nearly imperceptible.

Kids grow. Their bodies get bigger and stronger allowing them to explore new heights and horizons. Their minds grow as they begin to develop cognitive thought processes. They are adapting to their environment and growing as individuals. The problem is that many parents never adapt with them. They continue to employ the same *'telling'* parenting strategy.

Note: Parenting should have the same disclaimer as investment brokers... *Past results are not a guarantee of future results.* In life and in business, you need to adapt to the circumstances and people in present day terms, not the past.

In many cases parents think kids are rebelling. Most often it is just a person not responding to the same parenting technique that was used on them as a toddler. Think about it.

What is the same about anyone as when they were a toddler? Do they still eat the same food? Do they wear the same clothes? Do they laugh at the same silly songs and shows? Do they think or act the same as they did when they were a toddler? If not, why would you employ the same parenting techniques and expect results? The answer is that most people haven't learned a better method.

Kids must feel significant. Like adults, they have thoughts and opinions. They have a world view that is unique to their limited scope of knowledge and experience. Just because their outlook may be based on different criteria than yours, doesn't make it any less valid. It is their viewpoint and should be respected as such.

This is the starting point for Secret #9 – Talk *with* Your Kids, Not *To* Your Kids.

Rather than lecturing them, try having a discussion with your kids. Take a page from their playbook and ask them questions.
Why did...?
How did you...?
How do you feel when you...?

You'll be amazed the level of conversation you'll have with kids even as young as five or six years old.

The key is to keep the questions coming and encourage them to keep asking you. This enables you to learn what's on their minds, how they're seeing things, and how they're interpreting what they're learning.

Secret #9 works hand-in-hand with *Secret #5 - Decisions Have Consequences*. Discuss with your kids their goals and responsibilities. Chat about your expectations of them and their expectations for themselves. Allow them some ownership over their own decisions. Ask what they believe should be their rewards for achieving a goal or completing a responsibility. You can also ask what the consequences should be for negative actions.

Remember that because they're not your '*Mini-Me*' what you choose as a reward or punishment may not mean much to them. It may surprise you how well their choices motivate them. Keep in mind that as the adult you'll always have veto power over these choices. Talking "with" instead of "to" your kids will help in their identity discovery process.

For example, if they have a task to complete you can ask them when they think they'll have it done.
Parent: "*So you're saying you'll have this done by [then].*"

Kid: "*Yes.*"

Parent: "*Do you need anything from me, any help, to ensure you'll have it done by then?*"

Kid: "*No.*"

Parent: "*OK, so if you are finished, what should your reward be?*"

Kid: "*...*"
If it's a big goal they should get a bigger reward. If it's a small goal then a smaller reward is in order. And, the same should be true for the consequences.

For example when my kids have misbehaved in some way, shape or form, I'll ask them, *"What do you think is an appropriate punishment for this behavior?"* More often than not, they'll come up with a harsher punishment than I would have given out on my own. Sometimes I'll even say, *"Ya know I think that's a little too much. Let's scale that back a bit."*

Secret #10: Failure is NOT an Option.

This should be true for everyone. But most of the time it's not. Today, kids are often taught that failure is OK. They get A's for effort and a trophy for participating. In the real world, failure is not OK and successful achievement is rewarded.

By nature, kids are hardwired to succeed. Perseverance is an instinctive trait. For example, how many times does the average child try to walk before he or she gives up? They don't give up. They never give up. They do whatever it takes to get from here to there. They keep trying and trying and trying.

Even as babies they find a way to move themselves from one place to another. Because their legs aren't strong enough to support them they start with crawling, rolling, scooting, bouncing. Eventually, they build the necessary strength and they are off and running. A true success story if ever there was one. That drive to succeed is inside every child on the planet.

As parents we keep prodding them along. We keep encouraging them. It's an extremely natural thing, as human beings, for us to do. We want the best for them.

From birth we're all hard wired to succeed. That's Secret #10 – Failure Is Not an Option.

So, what changes? It's simple. **Kids learn to quit. Quitting is a learned behavior that they get from adults.** In fact, many adults have become so adept at quitting that they have streamlined the process into not even beginning. It's so much less work and bother that way. What lesson does that teach the children around them?

A perfect example of how we innately think for ourselves happened with my daughter. When she was about two years old we were at a restaurant. There was something on the table she wanted. She'd reach for it; I'd say "*no*" and move it and she'd reach for it again. Finally she dropped her spoon on the floor. That happens with toddlers, they drop stuff. I bent over to pick it up. When I came back up, she had reached over and grabbed what she'd wanted. She tricked me. I was so proud!

I know what you saying. What? Proud? You just got outsmarted by a two year old. Exactly. It was a classic misdirection-move like a magician would use and I am not ashamed to say I fell for it.

At only 2 years of age, she was thinking for herself and devised a way to get what she wanted. Failing, quitting simply wasn't even a known option to her. A trait that I am pleased to say has lasted into her teens and young adulthood.

Conclusion

There is an old saying: Knowledge is Power.

To that I say "***Bull$%@#!***"

Knowledge means nothing without application. If you don't use it, what good is it?

You are now armed with knowledge than can dramatically affect your life and the lives of those closest to you. What are you going to do with it?

Who are **YOU** going to **BE** today?

I AM...

A remarkable, thoughtful and passionate person who has an abundance of gifts to offer anyone who is willing to accept them

A messenger of happiness and success

A devoted husband who worships his wife more than she will ever know

A committed father who loves his children with the intensity of a thousand suns, and therefore must set the example for my children

A team player who will gladly sacrifice my own glory for the good of the team

I have flaws, and I am committed to overcoming those flaws so that I will have even more to give

Loved by those close to me - and I AM full of love and gratitude for those people being in my life

A billionaire...whose accounts have yet to be fully funded

A world class athlete

An attractive person – both physically and spiritually

Driven to achieve my definition of success

Disciplined to maintain the regimens I need to achieve my definition of success

A genius capable of creating things that change people's lives

THE VOICE

A LEADER

A CREATOR

A BELIEVER

A FORCE FOR GOOD

ONE WHO DEFIES THE ODDS

ONE WHO SETS NEW STANDARDS

I AM MARK PAPADAS

What professionally recognized thought leaders are saying about
I AM... 4 KIDS: 10 SECRETS TO EMPOWER KIDS & AWAKEN THE CHILD WITHIN YOU ~ By Mark Papadas.

"I love this book! Mark Papadas empowers kids and adults alike. He shares simple, life-changing techniques and thought processes that will transform your own life while you're teaching wonderful lessons to your children. This book is full of "Aha" moments. Thank you, Mark!"

- Barbara Niven
Actress, Speaker, Author, Hollywood's Top Media Coach

"I recommend I AM 4 Kids to every educational organization that is committed to developing strong minds, characters and bodies."

Randy Lawrence
Board Vice-President, Curriculum Committee Chair
Cary Community Consolidated School District 26

"Whether a child is 10 years old, or 20 or 40, it is always the right time to give them the gift of empowerment."

- Mrs. Rona Simmons
Elementary School Principal

"I have been a social worker for 15 years. I am also a mother of three (ages 10, 9, & 6). I AM 4 Kids is unique in that it reaches children at a crucial, developmental time in their lives. This system builds a child's sense of self worth while his/her identity is in such a critical, formative stage. I can't wait to start using it with my students in my district & my children at home."

Tracy M. Walsh, MSW, LSW
Public School Social Worker

"As a psychologist with over 35 years of experience doing therapy, and as a father of two grown children, I can honestly say that I wish my children had the benefit of I AM 4 Kids when they were in grade school. I highly recommend this book."

Timothy J. Hayes, Psy.D.
Licensed Clinical Psychologist

"Mark Papadas provides an amazing vehicle for kids to look at their life, mapping out a mission, and allowing them the creativity and freedom to move forward."

– Chuck Schultz
Personal Development Expert
Robbins Research International Master Trainer

"Mark Papadas is an inspiration! His mission is infectious, and he is leaving a legacy of extraordinary value to the world."

- Sarah Victory
Author, Speaker, Consultant, Media Personality
President, The Victory Company, Inc.